MIGHTY ANIMAL MIGRATIONS

A SALMON'S JOURNEY

David and Julie Lavender

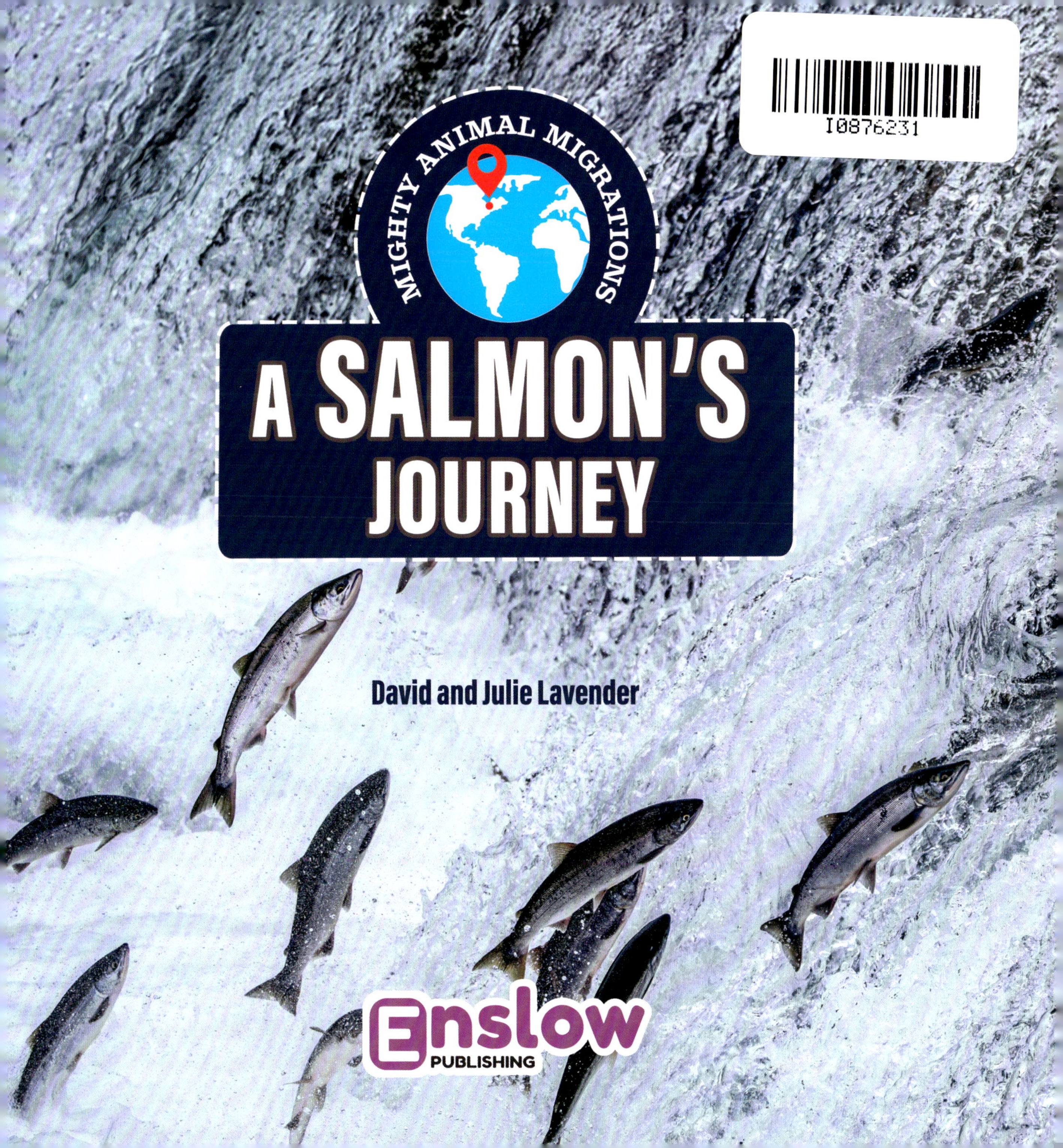

Enslow PUBLISHING

Please visit our website, www.enslow.com. For a free color catalog of all our high-quality books,
call toll free 1-800-398-2504 or fax 1-877-980-4454

Published in 2027 by
Enslow Publishing
2544 Clinton Street
Buffalo, NY 14224

Cataloging-in-Publication Data
Names: Lavender, David R., 1961-, author. | Lavender, Julie, author.
Title: A salmon's journey / by David and Julie Lavender.
Description: Buffalo, NY : Enslow Publishing, 2027. | Series: Mighty animal migrations | Includes glossary.
Identifiers: ISBN 9781978549609 (pbk.) | ISBN 9781978549616 (library bound) | ISBN 9781978549623 (ebook)
Subjects: LCSH: Salmon--Migration--Juvenile literature.
Classification: LCC QL638.S2 L384 2027 | DDC 597.561568--dc23

Photo credits: Cover, p 1, lfkdsk/Shutterstock.com; Calendars used throught interior, Evolvect/AdobeStock.com; blue background used throughout interior, arva/AdobeStock.com; p 4, wildestanimal/Shutterstock.com; p 5, Beat J Korner/Shutterstock.com, Kevin Wells Photography/Shutterstock.com; p 6, Jeremy Wood Photography/Shutterstock.com; p 7, Watthana Tirahimonchan/Shutterstock.com; p 8, Harry Collins Photography/Shutterstock.com; p 9, Zykov_Vladimir/Shutterstock.com; p 10, yamaoyaji/Shutterstock.com; p 11, picryl/Shutterstock.com; p 12, Steenstra/Shutterstock.com; p. 12 Peter @Wicki; p 13, Anatoliy Lukich/Shutterstock.com; p 14, KarepaStock/Shutterstock.com; p 15, Dominic Gentilcore PhD/Shutterstock.com; p 16, LouieLea/Shutterstock.com; p 17, leo w kowal/Shutterstock.com; p 18, SVITO-Time/Shutterstock.com; p 19, Everett Collection/Shutterstock.com, Keith Publicover/Shutterstock.com; p 20, slowmotiongli/Shutterstock.com; p 21 DoublePhoto Studio/Shutterstock.com; p 22, Lillian Tveit/Shutterstock.com; p 23, Finn Steiner/Shutterstock.com; p 24, Ronnie Chua/Shutterstock.com; p 25, oknemada1/Shutterstock.com; Sandris Kuzmickis/Shutterstock.com; p 27, Galyna Andrushko/Shutterstock.com; p 29 NOAA

Printed in China

CPSIA compliance information: Batch #QSENS27: For further information, contact Enslow Publishing, New York, New York, at 1-800-398-2504.

Table of Contents

Swimming Onward

Millions of animals migrate long distances every year. Some travel by land. Some swim through the sea. And others take to the air.

They set out on long, dangerous journeys in search of food or better living conditions. Sometimes animals migrate to find a mate or a place to give birth.

Atlantic salmon migrate from freshwater streams to the ocean. There, they grow bigger and gain the energy needed to lay eggs. Then, they migrate back to their freshwater homes to **spawn**.

Atlantic salmon

Pacific salmon

Salmon Tales

Atlantic salmon and Pacific salmon are both in the same family. Seven types, or **species**, of Pacific salmon can be found in the Pacific Ocean. Only one species of Atlantic salmon lives in the Atlantic Ocean.

A Salmon is Born

One spring afternoon, a salmon hatches from an egg in Pleasant River, Maine. The tiny fish is surrounded by hundreds of other newly-hatched salmon.

The small salmon hides under tiny pebbles with the others. They wait in the nest at the bottom of the small stream for three or four weeks.

Then, the tiny fish pushes against the pebbles and swims out of the nest. She's hungry, and it's time to look for food!

salmon eggs

Salmon Tales

Scientists have different names for a salmon as it grows from one stage to another in its **life cycle**. It starts as an egg and becomes an alevin when it hatches. As it grows bigger, scientists call it a fry, parr, smolt, and adult.

Eat, But Don't Get Eaten

The little fry is only one inch (2.5 cm) long. She feeds on tiny **organisms** so small they can only be seen with a microscope.

Soon she can eat small mayflies, stoneflies, blackflies, and beetles. Between each bite, she watches out for swimming bass and pike that want a yummy snack. Suddenly, an osprey swoops close to the water and nabs a nearby fish with its sharp claws. That was a close call for the little salmon!

An otter steps into the stream, and the salmon fry hides. Life is dangerous for a small fish.

osprey

SUMMER
alevin hatching

Changes

The fry soon grows to be two inches (5 cm) long. It develops vertical markings with a red dot between them. Now, she's called a parr. The little parr keeps eating and growing.

Summer passes. Then autumn, winter, and spring. She's a year old, but it's not time to leave the river just yet. She'll live for another year in the river and grow to be eight inches (20 cm) long.

« fry

2
YEARS
parr

Even More Changes

The little salmon's body makes big changes after two years in the freshwater river. Her back darkens. The vertical markings change to a silver shine.

Her **gills** change in preparation for heading to the ocean. Some of the organs inside her body change to handle life in salt water. The young salmon is called a smolt now.

It's time for the big migration!

« smolt

SPRING

Salmon Tales

Salmon are **anadromous** fish. That's a big word that means they migrate from fresh water to the ocean. They spend most of their lives in the ocean. Then, they return to fresh water to lay eggs.

Heading Out to Sea

The smolt starts her migration journey in the spring. She swims downriver. The river gets wider and wider and soon meets the Atlantic Ocean. On the journey, the young salmon collects smells for her memory bank. She'll need this information when she returns to spawn.

Salmon use **instinct** to navigate an epic migration journey from their river home to their new home in the ocean thousands of miles away.

When the young salmon reaches the ocean, she heads north through the Gulf of Maine. She swims miles and miles to get to the Labrador Sea. She'll spend her first summer, autumn, and winter here.

1
YEAR

Salmon Tales

Unfortunately, humans have blocked many of the paths for migrating salmon. Dams and power plants sometimes block rivers for young salmon swimming downstream and adult salmon swimming back upstream. Many salmon won't survive.

The fish ladder at John Day Dam provides passage upstream for salmon.

Eat. Grow. Repeat.

The young salmon spends her days dining on the ocean's buffet of prey. She sneaks up on small fish like sardines and herring. She gobbles up mouthfuls of **krill**. She munches on small squid. She even slurps up a sea worm.

The purpose of the salmon's migration is to grow big and healthy. Plenty of food in the ocean helps her grow fast. The bigger she is, the less likely she'll get eaten. She will also produce more eggs.

Eat. Grow. Repeat. Day after day after day.

krill

WINTER

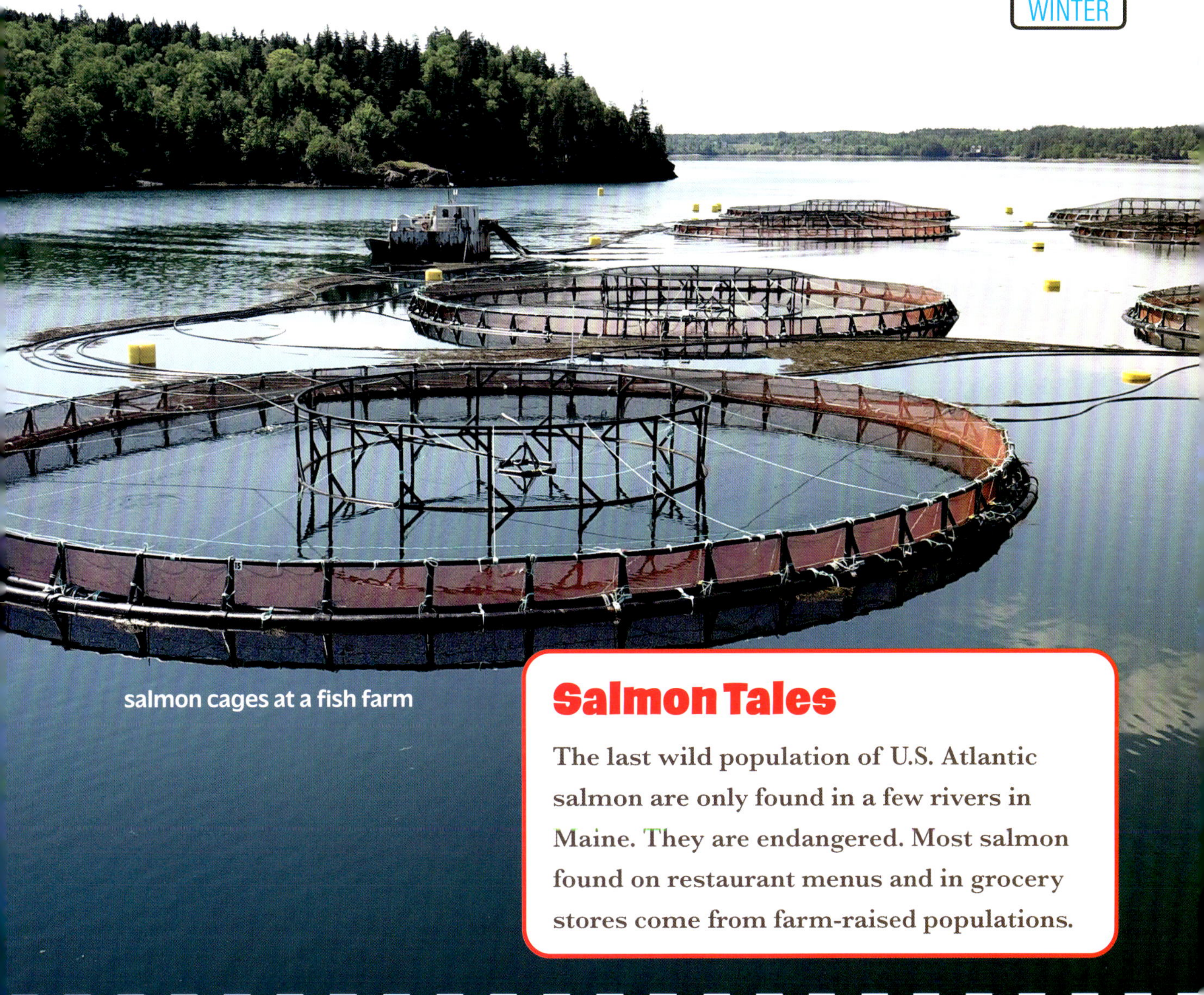

salmon cages at a fish farm

Salmon Tales

The last wild population of U.S. Atlantic salmon are only found in a few rivers in Maine. They are endangered. Most salmon found on restaurant menus and in grocery stores come from farm-raised populations.

Predator Alert!

Plenty of food in the open ocean means there's plenty of predators lurking there too. The young salmon swims left when a large tuna swims her way, dodges right when a swordfish moves forward, and ducks deeper when a striped bass swims by.

She hides from sharks. She watches out for seabirds and seals. And she stays away from killer whales, dolphins, and porpoises. It's not easy being a little fish in big waters.

The young salmon swims farther north for her second year at sea. She travels to the seas of Newfoundland and Greenland.

swordfish

Salmon Tales

Fishermen used to have contests to see who could catch the biggest salmon. One winner sent his 11-pound (5-kg) prize fish to President Taft in 1912. This started a yearly salmon tradition that lasted for 80 years! It ended in 1992 because so few wild salmon remained.

President Taft

Fresh Water Ahead

After two years in the ocean, the four-year-old adult salmon knows it's time to migrate home. She heads south. When a dark shadow passes overhead, the salmon swishes her fins faster and faster. A killer whale swims faster too, hoping for lunch. The salmon barely escapes.

Days turn into weeks. The salmon just keeps swimming. When she reaches Pleasant Bay, Maine, her instincts kick in. She remembers this part of the journey.

Suddenly, a gray seal leaps into the water and nips the salmon's tail. The salmon jerks to the left and then to the right. The salmon escapes. She quickly heads up the river.

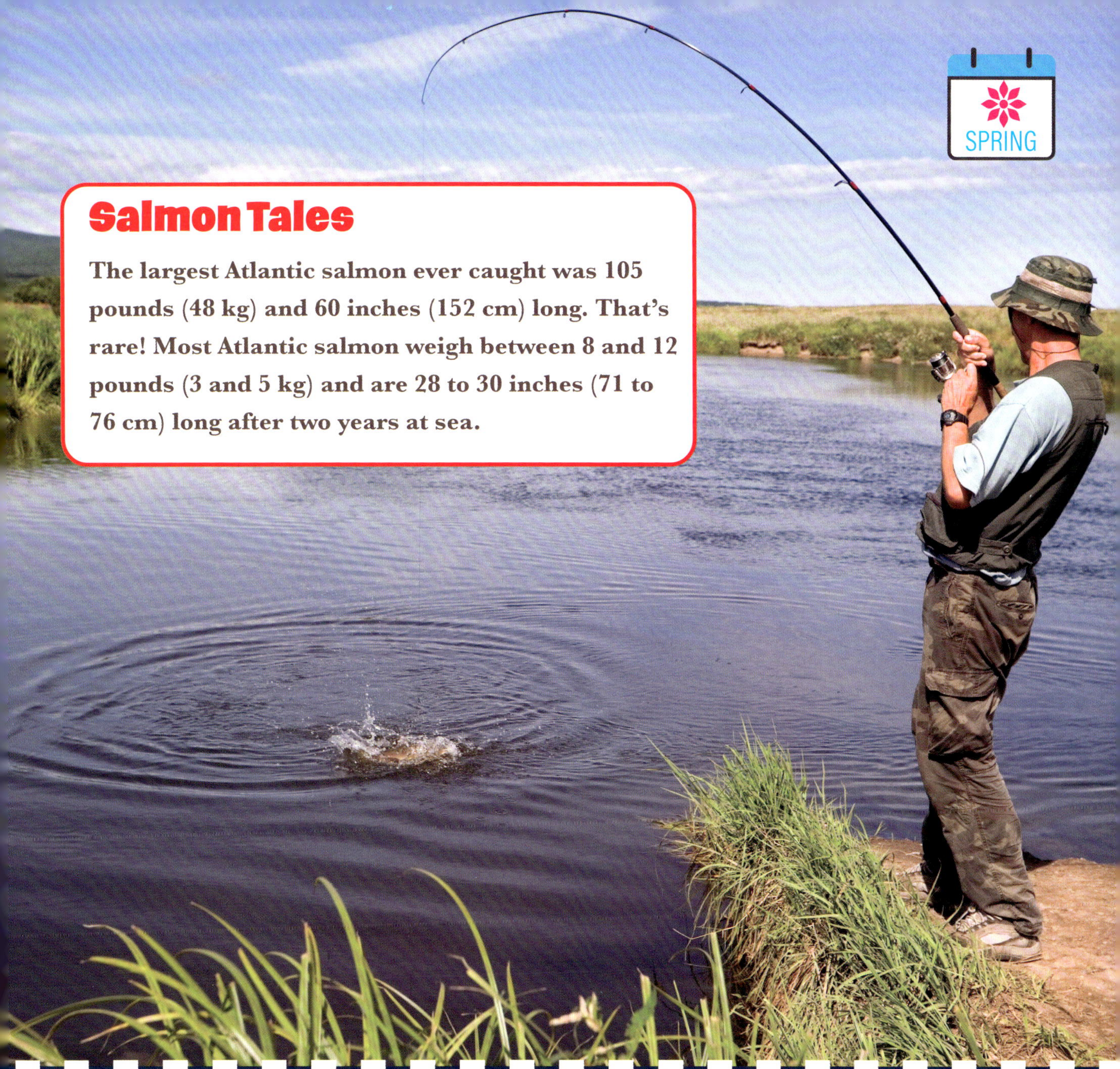

Salmon Tales

The largest Atlantic salmon ever caught was 105 pounds (48 kg) and 60 inches (152 cm) long. That's rare! Most Atlantic salmon weigh between 8 and 12 pounds (3 and 5 kg) and are 28 to 30 inches (71 to 76 cm) long after two years at sea.

Bear-ly Able to Escape

After returning to fresh water, the salmon stops hunting for food. She spends her energy swimming home to spawn. She uses her sense of smell and memory to travel back to the place where she hatched.

It's hard to swim upstream. The current is swift. She pushes harder. She leaps out of the water to jump over rapids. The salmon springs forward to get over a waterfall.

Claws grab her in mid-air. A black bear! The salmon twists and turns. She jerks and pushes. She slips out of the bear's paw and lands back in the water with a *SPLASH*!

SUMMER

Salmon Tales

It's hard for humans to understand just how animals know where to go to migrate. Because Earth is like a giant magnet, animals like salmon use the pull of Earth's magnetic field to guide them like a compass.

Home, Sweet Home

The salmon pushes harder with her fins. She swishes her tail faster. Finally, the salmon is home. She's back to the very same spot in the river where she hatched. The salmon makes a nest in the bottom of the stream. She lays about 6,000 eggs that her body formed while out at sea.

A male salmon swimming nearby **fertilizes** the eggs. Then, the female salmon swishes her tail to cover the eggs with rocks and gravel. The eggs remain in the nest all winter until they hatch next spring.

The salmon's job is done. Soon, the cycle will start all over. With a push of her tail, she's heading downstream. It's time for another migration.

Salmon Tales

To form a nest, a female salmon swishes its tail rapidly to move dirt and gravel from the bottom of the stream. She makes the hole about one foot (30 cm) deep. It has to be big enough to hold a lot of eggs!

The Salmon Migration

Wild Atlantic salmon take part in an epic migration of almost 6,000 miles (9,700 km). These endangered animals hatch in a river in Maine. They travel all the way to the coasts of Newfoundland and Greenland.

When it's time to lay eggs, these amazing fish use instinct, smell, and magnetic cues to guide them back to their freshwater home.

It's a hard journey with man-made dangers and predators around every bend. Some won't survive. But others will make the journey again and again.

A Salmon Migration Map

1. A salmon hatches from an egg in Pleasant River, Maine.
2. She swims and eats and grows in the river for two years.
3. The salmon swims downriver toward the Atlantic Ocean.
4. She heads north through the Gulf of Maine.
5. After miles and miles of swimming, the salmon reaches the Labrador Sea.
6. She swims and eats and grows in the Labrador Sea for a year.
7. The salmon swims farther north to the seas of Newfoundland and Greenland. She stays another year at sea.
8. After two years at sea, the salmon swims south.
9. She makes her way to the Labrador Sea.
10. The salmon swims through the Gulf of Maine.
11. Once the salmon reaches the Pleasant River, she'll swim north.
12. The salmon swims all the way back to the very spot where she hatched from an egg.

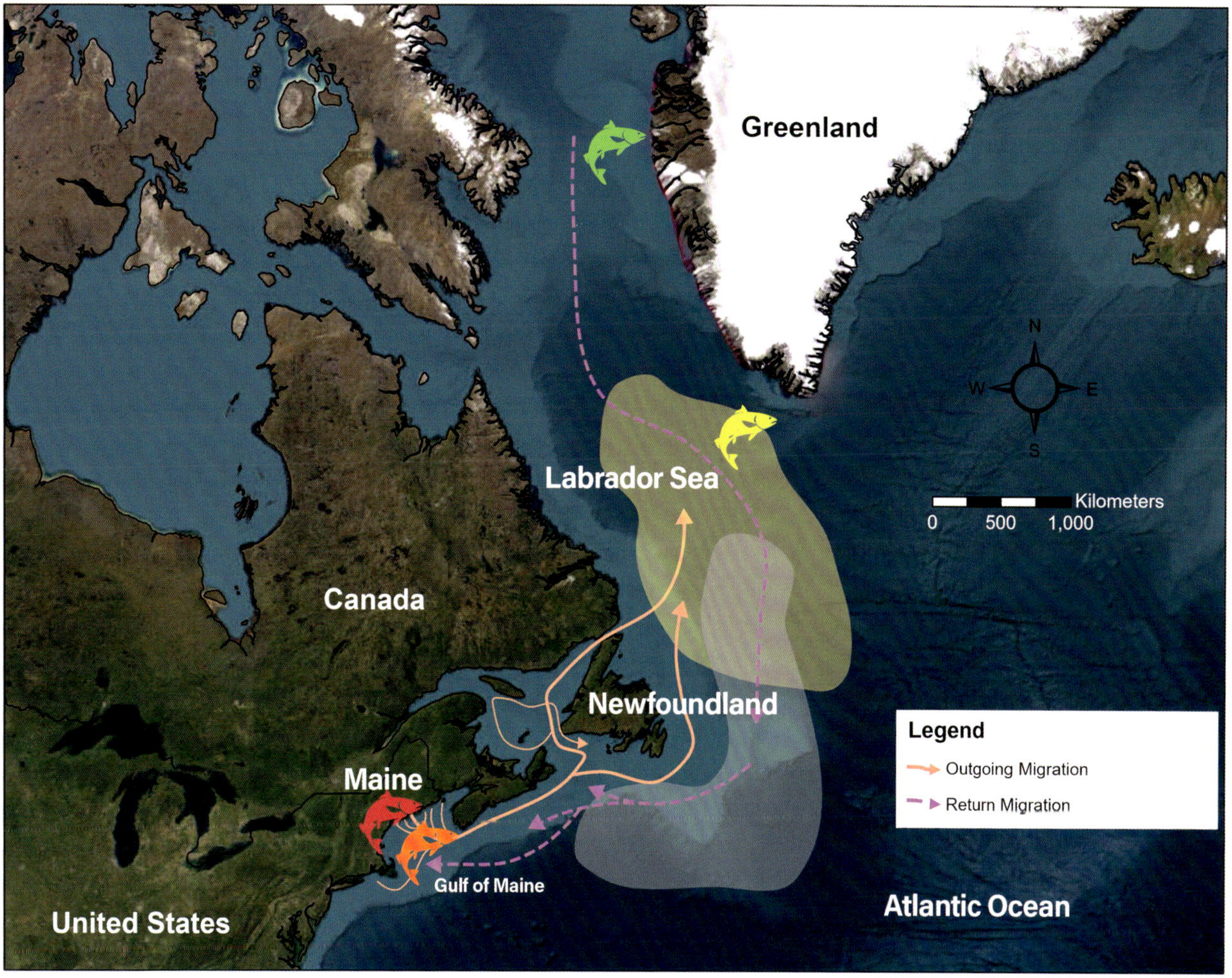
Greenland
N
W
E
S
Labrador Sea
Kilometers
0 500 1,000
Canada
Newfoundland
Legend
Outgoing Migration
Return Migration
Maine
Gulf of Maine
United States
Atlantic Ocean

Glossary

anadromous (uh-NA-druh-muhs): a life cycle where a fish migrates from fresh water to salt water to grow and then migrates back to their freshwater home to lay eggs

fertilizes (FUR-tuh-lye-ziz): the first step in producing young

gills (gilz): the organs on a fish's head through which it breathes

instinct (IN-stingkt): behavior that is natural and not learned

krill (kril): tiny shrimplike creatures that live in the ocean and are an important food source for many animals

life cycle (life SYE-kuhl): the series of changes a living thing goes through from birth to death

organisms (OR-guh-niz-uhmz): living things

spawn (spawn): to produce a large number of eggs

species (SPEE-sheez): a group of living things that are alike and can produce young together

Fact Check

1. Wild Atlantic salmon start their life as an egg laid in a ____ stream in Maine.

   a. freshwater b. fast-moving c. polluted

2. Atlantic salmon migrate from Maine to the coasts of Newfoundland and ____.

   a. Greenland b. Canada c. Mexico

3. Atlantic salmon use memory and their sense of _______ to find the way back to fresh water to spawn.

   a. hearing b. smell c. sight

Answers: 1. a, 2. a, 3. b

Further Reading

Accardi, Anne. *Celebrating the Chinook Tribes*. Mitchell Lane Publishing, 2026.

Murray, Julie. *Animals in Streams & Rivers*. ABDO Publishing Company, 2021.

Rice, Jamie. *A Salmon's Life Cycle*. Jump!, Inc., 2022.

On the Internet

An Incredible Journey

www.fisheries.noaa.gov/west-coast/outreach-and-education/incredible-journey-series-educational-resources-promote-salmon-stewardship

Learn more about Pacific salmon with a picture book, fun game, and life cycle video.

The Salmon Life Cycle

www.nps.gov/olym/learn/nature/the-salmon-life-cycle.htm

Read about a salmon's life cycle from fry to smolt to adult.

Publisher's note to educators and parents: Our editors have carefully reviewed these websites to ensure that they are suitable for students. Many websites change frequently, however, and we cannot guarantee that a site's future contents will continue to meet our high standards of quality and educational value. Be advised that students should be closely supervised whenever they access the internet.

Index

About the Authors

David and Julie Lavender loved watching Pacific salmon swim in streams when they lived in Washington State, but they've never seen wild Atlantic salmon before. David enjoyed working with lots of different kinds of animals, first as an entomologist and then as a wildlife biologist. Julie enjoyed teaching public school kids and then their own children as a homeschooling mom. They love learning about animals and writing about them. Julie and David have written books for kids about sharks, insects, hidden treasure, and a picture book called *A Gingerbread House*. They have four adult kids and three grandchildren.